Thoughts Collected
Poetry

Devlin Murphy

Dedication

To my Daughters,

My greatest gifts and sweetest blessings.

To those I love —

You know who you are…

Prologue

I have traveled many paths and all have led me here. I've shed tears of sadness and joy along the way. I have scars, some you can see and some you can't. Through it all I've played with words. One word can create an image, a feeling, a though, a portrait. The play of words, pictures painted, a sensory of sound and cadence… come along and read. Open your mind, your heart, and your ears. Come see what you can hear.

Awake
alive
another to die
always moving
never rested.
Always asking why?
Living life unfulfilled
Withered thrills.
Here's a pill
One step forward
One step back
Another day
Under attack
What do I lack?
Bought the lie
To live like
I'll never die
Bought societies dogma
That I need everything
To succeed
To survive
To thrive
Be thin
be beautiful
be wealthy
be hip
be young
I'm done.
Be something unachievable
And wonder why...
I cry
I stand alone
On my rock

Devlin Murphy

I will not buy the lie anymore.
I am enough
As I am
If it bothers
I don't give a damn
This is where I make my
Stand-
I am good enough
As I am.

I am a Woman
I laugh
I cry
I am strong
I am weak
I work
I play
I am a Mother
I am a daughter
I am a granddaughter
I am a niece
I am a cousin
I am an ex-wife
I am a Teacher
I am a giver
I am a lover
I am a bitch
I get things done
I don't waste time
I am learned
I read
I write
I think
I fight
I have pain
I have scars
I have heart
I am kind
I am fierce
I am a Warrior
I am hopeful

I talk
I live
I love
I dream
I am a Woman

Devlin Murphy

I am fearful
I am found
I am lost
I am a wanderer
I am interested
I am interesting
I am beautiful
I am a hag
I am loyal
I am reliable
I've birthed
I've survived
I walk
Kindred Spirits
Open hearts
Laughter flows
Histories shared
Feelings spared
Give and take
Never false
Never fake
Best friends do make.

Bitter Dreams

Hopes fade
reality looms
relentless pursuit
ideas wither
repeat plays
Hopes fade
longings burn
desire wanes
ashes scatter
swallowing bile
Bitter Dreams
Time passes
images fade
desires wanes
hopes remain
again, again
we start anew
failing, failures
see us through
time passes
beauty fades
lust dims

Devlin Murphy

Finally
Time
Arrives
Changes
Discipline
Absolute
Self
Reclaims
broken
Unyielding
Resilient
Fortitude

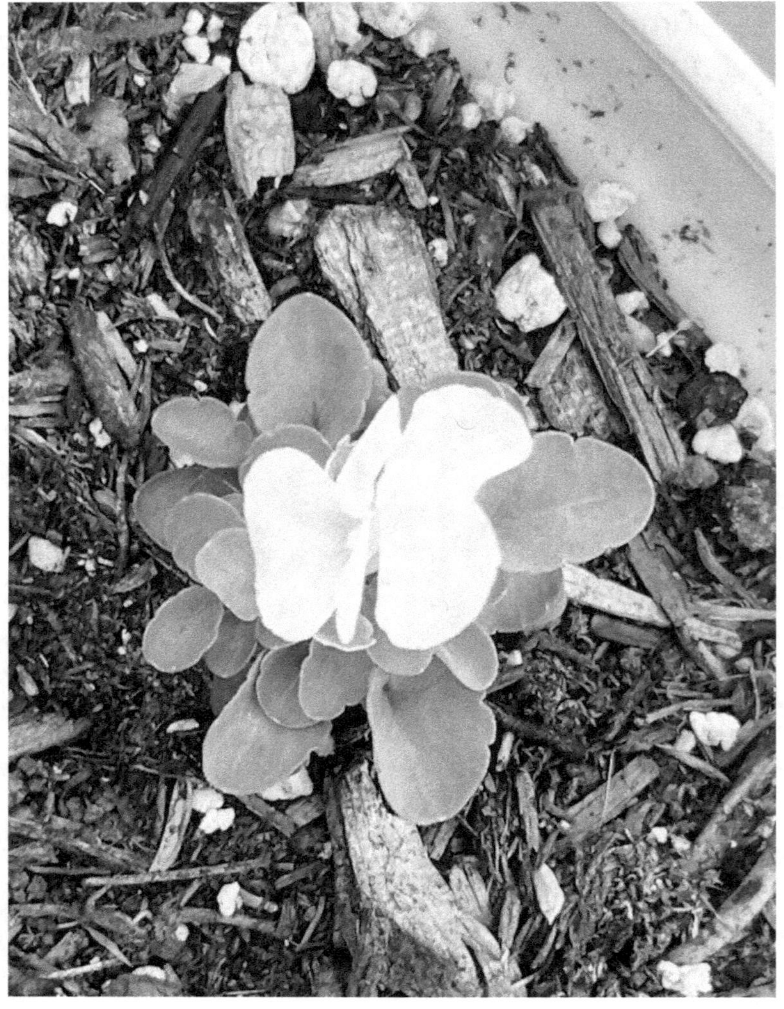

Devlin Murphy

What magic can madness wrought?

Endless possibilities
Endless equations
Endless roads
Endless paths
endless..........

Dead Roses

Sweet flowers blooming
raise their lovely faces towards the sun.
Precious time to bloom gracefully
only to wither and die.
Is there a sadder sight to see
then Dead Roses.

Is this our story?
Mortal-beings born and grow
some bloom beautifully....
Precious time to learn and grow
only to wither and die
Is there a sadder sight to see
then Dead Roses.

There is a beginning
and an end.
Precious time used, abused or even
wasted
only to wither and die
Is there a sadder sight to see
then Dead Roses....

Devlin Murphy

limits
limitless
dreams
dreamless
hope
hopeless
useful
useless
used
love
loveless
point
pointless

I scream in my useless dreams
I dream in my useless life
I hope in my withered spirit
I fight in my broken self
to find the joy
to find the freedom
to find the creative force
to find the hope...
again....

11

selfishness
selfless
same?

Devlin Murphy

Rain
Split, splat
Takes me away
Hypnotized
Split, splat
Tears
of joy
of sorrow
Do the clouds
cry?
I wonder
I dream
through the drops
When will it
Stop
Good mood
Bad mood
Depends on the day.
Split, splat
Let the
rain play

Dreams of future
Flashbacks of past
Drowning in present
When....
Change....
Joy.....
Love.....
Dreams of hope
Flashbacks of pain
Numb in present.

Devlin Murphy

14

Time is now
Now is time
It flys
It crawls
It goes
It stops

What is my CORE-Who AM I?

I am a strong woman
I am fearless, mostly
I am joyful
I am funny
I am playful
I am kind
I am interesting
I am a doer
I am gentle
I am a fighter
I am intelligent
I am a thinker
I am a learned woman
I am deep
I am spiritual
I am resilient
I am true
I am fair
I am love
I am passionate
I am a warrior
I am honorable
I am a no bullshit zone
I am capable
I am a bitch
Don't fuck with me
I fuck back.

Devlin Murphy

LIFE…

Is precious
Is fleeting
Is fragile
Is strong
Is long
Is short
Is predictable
Is chaos
Is joyful
Is heartbreak
Is health
Is illness
Is laughter
Is serious
Is playful
Is work
Is passion
Is regret
Is thoughtful
Is cruel
Is safe
Is scary
Is plentiful
Is scarce
Is easy

Is hard
Is all
Is nothing
Is here
Is gone
Is now
LIVE…

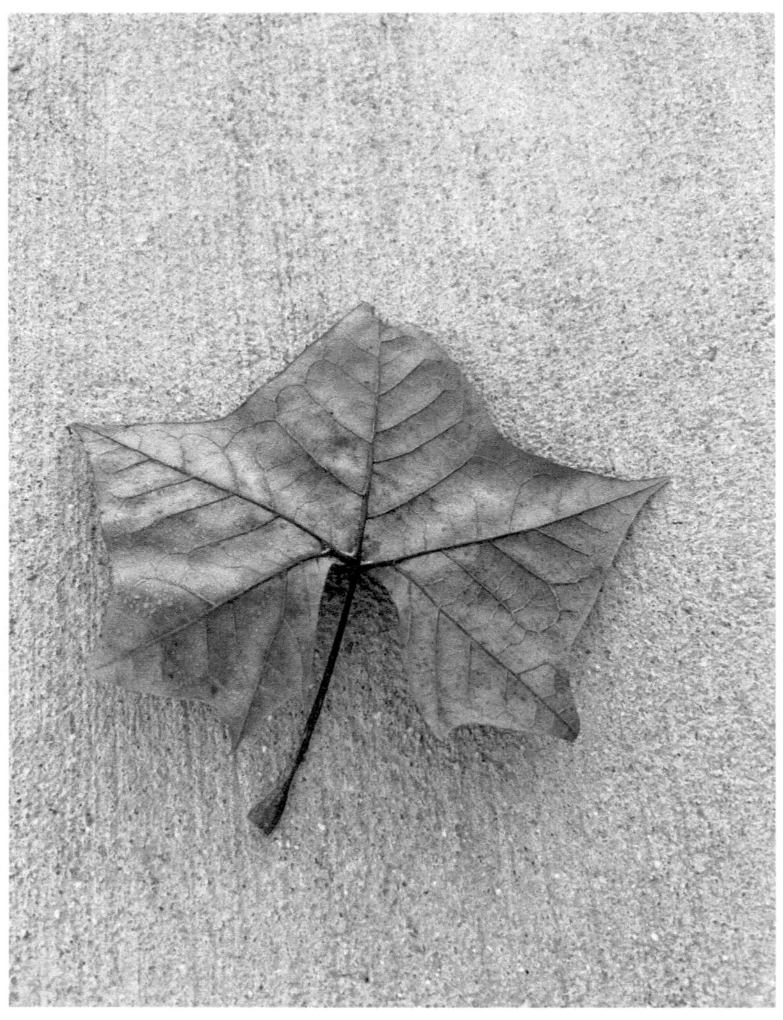

Devlin Murphy

Dangerous days
Dangerous nights
Longing for changing
No effort given
I want what I want
No work involved
Changes-
Smanges-
Off-again-
Yes-no
Right-wrong
Does anything matter,
anything at all.
Nothing and no one
Alone and gone
Here and there
Over and done
Another day
Lost to indifference
Another day lost to
The mundane
Archaic
Meaningless
Useless
Lost and lonely-
Devoid of life-
We laugh
We drink
We pee
We eat
We sleep
Do we live?
Do we really live?
I am not afraid of dying.
I'm afraid I won't get to live...

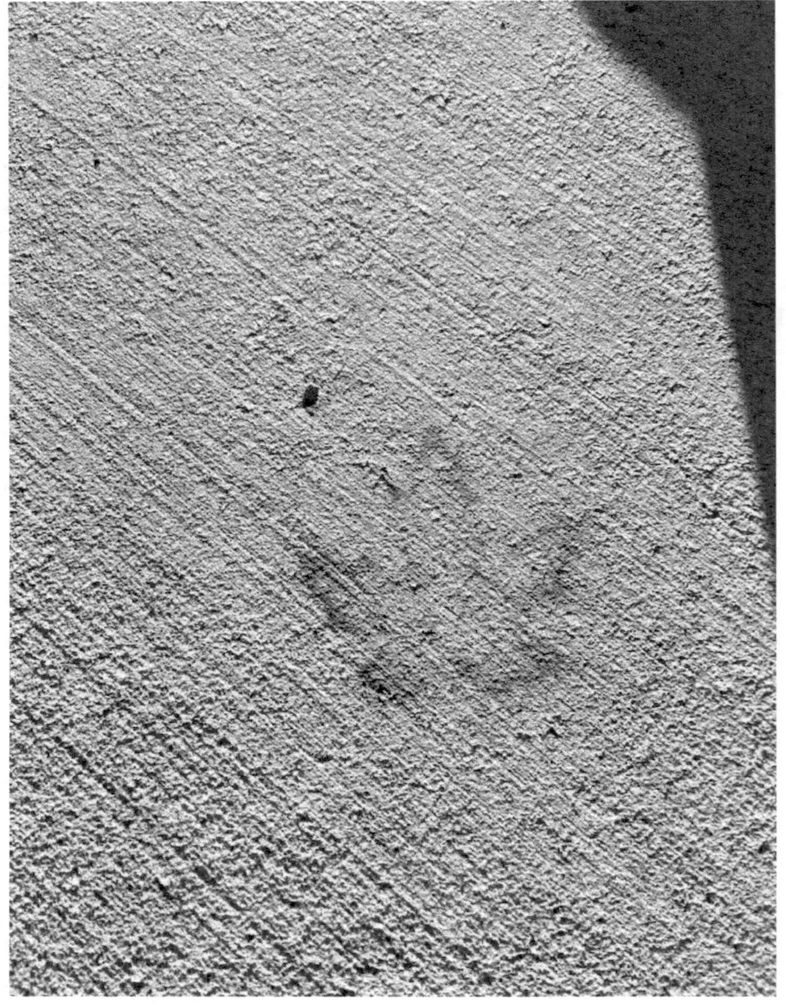

Devlin Murphy

I am ready to love again.
I will begin with me.
Years of heartbreak
Melting away.
Like new buds
I will bloom again.
I will dare to be me.
I will free my voice.
I will muster the courage to
Live again.

Dreaming to be free
Already am...
Dreaming to love
Already do....
Dreaming to be whole
A work in progress
Dreaming to create
Already...

Devlin Murphy

I am tired
Tired of wishing
Tired of failing
Tired of waiting
Tired of settling
Tired of struggling
Tired of fighting
Tired of dreaming
Tired of stress
Tired of anger
Tired of excuses
I am alive
Alive to possibilities
Alive to change
Alive to hope
Alive to believe
Alive to change
Alive to thrive
Alive to dream
Alive to action
Alive to do
Alive to love
I am Ready.

Racing Heart
Stagnate Start
Vision cleared
Truth unfolded

Devlin Murphy

Rainbows Rise
Surprise
Guide
It is my time
To Rise
Surprise
Guide

25

My Dear Friend,

Handsome
Gentleman
Scholar
Kind
Generous
Funny
Irrepressible
Irreplaceable
My Friend,
I love you.

Devlin Murphy

It's now
Time to shine
Let the light
Time to shine
Time to cut
Again
Pain either way
If I live
I write
I'll write my way out~
Yes, Hamilton...
I am ready to take
My shot
Twenty five years
Gone~
I will be heard
I will share my stories
Someone will listen?

It is right
That I write
It slides
It glides
It weaves
Its own web
I am just
The head
The pen
Waits
Mates
And the dance
Begins
I feel
I heal
I rage
At the cage
Freedom whispers...
I am here...

Devlin Murphy

Thoughts rise
Thoughts fly
Wondering why
Waves
A cyclical pace
Always out
Of place
Dreaming dreams
Washed away
By the mundane.
It starts again
It begs
It pleads
It bleeds
It is right
It is mine
Wandering waves
Start the day.

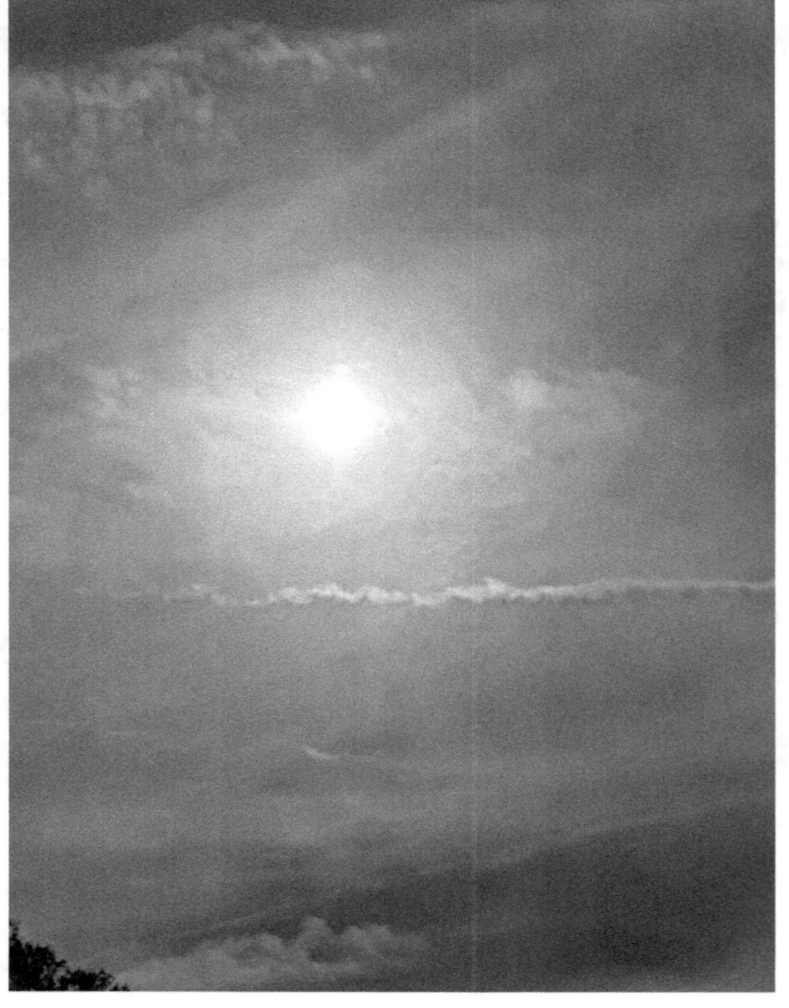

Devlin Murphy

The fear is done
I think I've won
I am ready
Turning pages
Let my
Ink strokes
Tell their
Story
In release
Find glory
Gory life
Filled with strife
Ready
To fight
I know
I'm right
I've got what it takes
I've been given
A break
Time to make
Create
I am.

I feel the wind
Against my face
My legs pump
Ground flys
Freedom
Freedom within
Freedom without
A fire rages
Time to
Turn pages
Create
Relate

32

Alive
Aware
Awake
Believe
Can
Do
Everything
Ha

Neediness
Constant
Attitudes
Constant
Cell phones
Constant
Excuses
Constant
Exceptions
Constant
Laziness
Constant
Demands
Constant
Repeat
Constant
Apathy
Constant
Why
Constant
Teacher
It's almost done
Another year
Another class
Unites young
Divided Country
Released
Into adulthood
By and by

A good lot
Drop it like its hot
Year in
Year out
Day in
Day out
Summer
The wheels
on the bus
round & round.

Devlin Murphy

Blah, blah, blah
So the story goes
The hour of discontent
Reigns in the hearts of good
men.
Chased out of a noble
calling by
incompetence and
indifference
Failed systems
False blame
a given
A season to remember
For who will teach
The children now?
I cannot take the blame
It is your shame
It will be all of our pain...
Now who's to blame?
I cannot raise your child
I cannot teach or parent
alone...

The children come to me at first light
Some with delight
Others a fright
Sleepy or pissy
Pleasant or grumpy
They take their seats
The music, the bell, the pledge
Are you awake?
Will you shut up?
Will you put down the phone?
Will you ever listen?

Lonely heart
Reaching out
Empty spaces
Blank places
Unknown faces
Hollow and alone
Holding on
Trodding along
Reasons abound
Low to the ground
Lonely heart
Holds hope
Splinters, frayed
Waylaid

Tears form
Do not flow
Mind reels
Cannot let go
Desire surges
Cannot be slaked
Injustice flames
Cannot be tamed
Unknown reasons
Elude my eyes
I sparkle
Then slowly die
Always asking why
Lonliness looms
There is no escape
Plans that never take
Questions ~ answers
All the same
Wallow in pain
Encrusted in shame
Ache for love
Always the same
Curse the sky
Always, why.....

Devlin Murphy

Breezes caress
Flowers bloom
Dog races
Heart beats
Soul settles
At peace
Always seeking
Answers, questions
Meaning...
Know
That I do not
Know
Dreams of my lovers kiss
Tastes of passion
The sights and smells
Awakened the senses
Warmth washes over
Hope springs ahead
I wander
I wonder
I live again

Time ticks by
Dreams fly
Hopes likes
Waves-builds
Crashes-builds
Longings unfulfilled
Undiminished
I rise again
I try again
I hope again
I breathe again
I write again
Undiminished
Through swamps
Of tears
And broken dreams
Betrayals
Faithless men
Useless friends
Undiminished
Endure
And rise again
Slumber well
And begin
Again
Undiminished...

Devlin Murphy

Angry voices
Long rooted hatred
Suffrage
Equality
The fight
Battles still rage
The chance
The voice
The hope
Hillary...

Choices
Good ones
Bad ones
Do overs
Choices
Time I've wasted
Time and time again
Moments lost
Moments gained
Money made
Money spent
Wasted
Enjoyed
Squandered
Saved
Time and time again
Love lost
Love given
Love taken
Love frozen
Lonliness
Oozes
Time ticks
Heart aches
Heart breaks
Heart beats
Heart hopes
Time...

Devlin Murphy

Foolishness
Foolish people
Pettiness
Petty people
Loneliness
Lonely people
Foulness
Foul people
Kindness
Kind people
Hopelessness
Hopeless people
Meanness
Mean people
Stupidness
Stupid people
Classiness
Classy people
What you get
Is what you give.

43

Anger oozes
False eyes
Easy lies
Personal affronts
Sold ambitions
Lazy steward
Jealous fool

Devlin Murphy

I dream of the future
I dream of the past
I dream of unknowns
I live the daily drudge
I live with the uncertainty
I live with hope
I accept the indifference
I accept the stupidity
I accept the selfishness
I wish for a life of peace
I wish for a life of meaning
I wish for a life of joy.

Humans crave
Humans destroy
Humans use
Humans abuse
Humans cry
Humans lie
Humans blame
Humans flame
Humans justify
Humans vilify
Humans waste
Humans taste
What is our fate.....

Devlin Murphy

They've come
They've gone
Some touched my heart
Some touched my nerves
All left a trace
I hope the best
For all of them
Some will soar
Some will flounder.

I try
I fail
I try again
I fail again
I shed a tear
For what might have been
I shed a few
For what has been
I wonder where, why, what
The future holds
Folly for sure
It is not for me to know.
I plan
I change
I adapt
I hold on
I stand up
I lie down
I wake up
And do it again.

Devlin Murphy

Stagnate and stale
Frustrated and afraid
Challenges and changes
Time takes its toll
When and whenever
Lost and lonely
Surrender and sacrifice
Days dissolve
Dreams die
Awake and arise
Try while time....

I wonder why
I squander time
I refuse to embrace joy
I seek
All
Wisdom, knowledge, meaning
Useless quests
When now is why
Now is what matters
The people, the place
The feeling within.
Why must I change
What is it?
What is it I reach for?
What is it that I do not already possess?
Changes
Needs
Work
Make it happen.

Devlin Murphy

Long for love
Must begin within
Seeking, searching
Wayward wanderings
Waylaid worth
Losing, lost
Timeless tirade
Faithless foolish
Scratching scars
Missing me
Deaf dreams
Endless seems
Journey's joy.

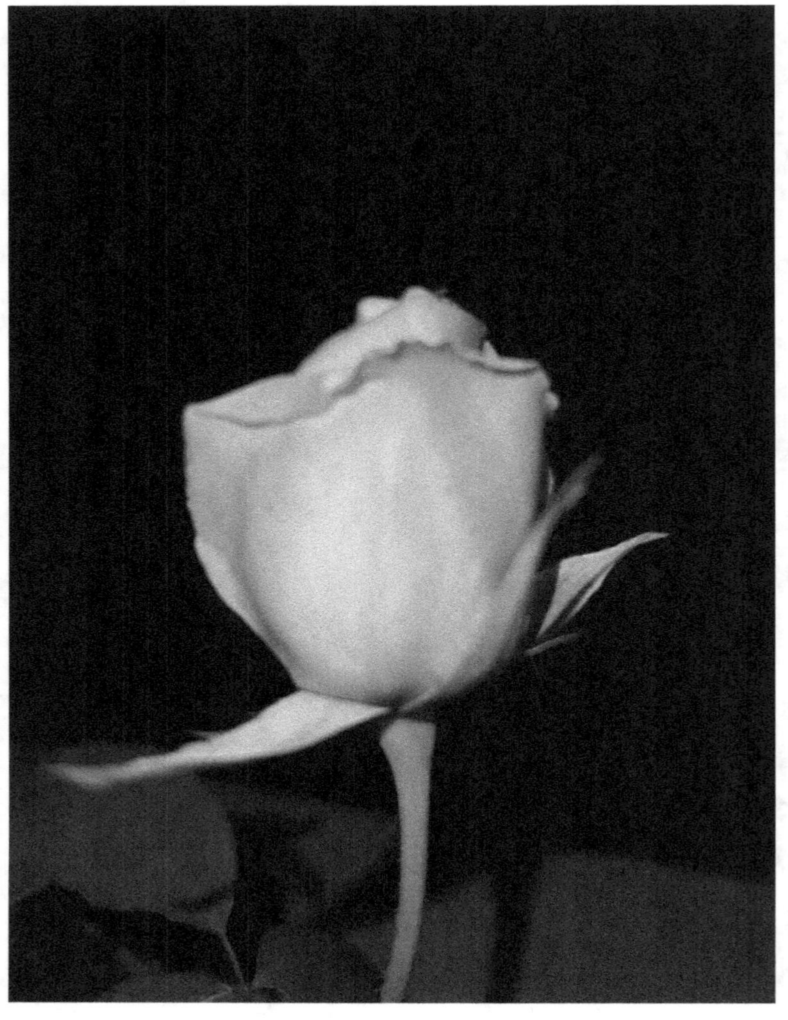

Devlin Murphy

Lost and lonely
struggling and insecure
worried, scared
scarred, charred
worthless, wounded
used, useless
frightened, alone
afraid, fearful
overweight and wasting away
drowning in doubt
swimming in alcohol
high on nicotine
no self control
spending money
can't buy love or worth
everything hurts.
tired
can't find my joy
can't find my feet
Trapped in confusion
passion gone
resentment brews
Ah hell,
Wake up!

A moment is approaching
The dawn of an awakening
Courage and fearlessness
To be brave and strong
Instead of afraid and weak
The path unfurls before me
Owning only ones choices
Decide...act...believe
The quest begins
The warrior awaits
Free her....
Words without action are worthless
Love thyself
Find thyself
Trust thyself
Be thyself
Free thyself
Time cleanses.

Devlin Murphy

Moments closing in.
Lost thoughts
Farewell to past mistakes
Looking forward
Holding hope
Deeds and decisions
Choices collide
Fragile pieces
Time to decide
Alone to carry the weight
Courage and faith
Endure and carry on
Whatever the fate.................

At the moments edge
Asking why
Demanding when
Knowing consequences
Finally accepting
Sweet voice of reason
Begs me to stay...
That simple request
Will change my life
Beginning...ending...
I love you
Enough to do what it takes...
I love you more than me
I can't or won't for me
For you;
I will fight
I will endure
I will sacrifice
I will survive
For you, always
My Daughters.

Devlin Murphy

Time has come
Time has stopped
Change must begin
Change from within
Lost and found
Gone to ground
So I rise again
Ashes to ashes
Strength
Determination
Resilient
Relentless
I will not surrender
I will never.

57

The time has come
Time to show up
Time to grow up
Time to do what must be done
Time to wash away the past
Time to release the future
Time to be me, now.

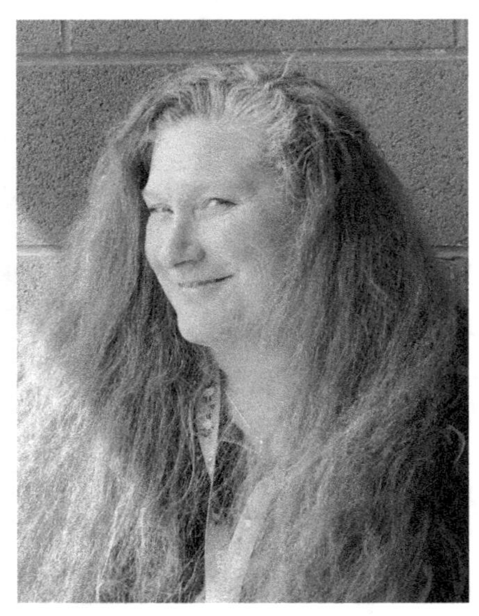

A mother
A teacher
A veteran
A poet
A woman
on a
journey

ThePagansPen.org